THE
LANDSCAPES
of EAST SUSSEX

RUPERT TAYLOR

– Photographs by –

DAVID SELLMAN

COUNTRYSIDE BOOKS
NEWBURY, BERKSHIRE

First published 2000
Photographs © David Sellman 2000
Text © Rupert Taylor 2000
Reprinted 2002

Countryside Books
3 Catherine Road
Newbury, Berkshire

To view our complete range of books,
please visit us at
www. countrysidebooks.co.uk

ISBN 1 85306 648 6

Produced through MRM Associates Ltd., Reading
Printed in Singapore

CONTENTS

Ashdown Forest

FOREWORD

God gives all men all earth to love,
But, since man's heart is small,
Ordains for each one spot shall prove
Beloved over all.
Each to his choice, and I rejoice
The lot has fallen to me
In a fair ground – in a fair ground –
Yea, Sussex by the sea!

Rudyard Kipling, *Sussex*

Sweet Sussex. She's not as rugged as some counties in England. She's not particularly wild. But here you will find, in miniature, all the beloved landscapes of the country blended in one brief but beautiful corner of the realm.

East is East and West is West, as the county's poet, Kipling, said. This book seeks out the delights of East Sussex: from the majestic coastline of mighty chalk and sandstone cliffs, to the fecund, womanly curves of naked downland; from the seething, life-rich flatlands of Pevensey Levels, to the sandy scrub acres of Ashdown Forest; from the man-made delights of tiny, flint villages and elegant seaside squares, to the shyest places of the deep, wooded Weald.

Set out to walk from the East Sussex coast and you could be in central London within a day. But here is a land as far removed from the City as you will find. There is no heavy industry. There is no motorway. The miles of dual carriageway you can almost count on two hands. Rustic rail lines take sleepy commuters to the capital.

The county keeps her secrets in the folds of a landscape whose gentle loveliness has been captured here by a brilliant series of pictures.

THE EVER CHANGING CAMBER SANDS

'Take that, Jerry! And that, and that, and that!'
John Mills in the film *Dunkirk* (1958)

A place of startling contrasts – from kiss-me-quick hats, ice creams and amusement arcades to majestic views, fascinating flora and glorious solitude. The sand dunes south-west of Camber village, the only ones in East Sussex, swarm with holidaymakers during the summer months. They are popular, too, with low budget TV and film crews in need of desert scenes.

Sea and wind combine to push the sand ashore and waft it inland where, lodged against rocks or trapped by vegetation, it gradually builds into mounds and ridges. It's an extraordinary landscape that's always on the move. Storms throw up new sand or suck back to the shore old deposits; as one ridge flattens out a new one begins to grow in front of it.

Salt, heat and bitter cold . . . it's a harsh environment for plants, but marram grass, sea holly, sea buckthorn and sea bindweed thrive here and lock the dunes together.

When the sunbathers and sandcastle architects have gone home, the humps and hillocks of Camber return to their own special charm, stretching down to the shoreline where the relentless sea continues its slow but sure process of constant change.

There's a bleak beauty here in the depths of winter as the gales sweep in from the English Channel and the sound of the crashing surf mingles with the cry of seabirds and the wind singing through the grasses.

A popular place in summer

Standing starkly apart from the holiday settlement is squat Camber Castle, the only 'Henrician' castle in Sussex – one built by Henry VIII when he feared invasion after his break with Rome. The castle was built on a peninsula to guard Rye Bay. Now a mile of shingle separates it from the sea.

The sea and the wind create Camber's shifting landscape

RYE – THE PORT LEFT BEHIND BY THE SEA

You soon forget the hazards of the cobbled streets in the sheer enchantment of your surroundings. It is hard to believe that there could be so much harmony in such a medley of bricks, tiles, stones and ancient timber.
Ben Darby, *Journey Through the Weald*

Rye perches quaint and comfortable on the sandstone outcrop which rises above the surrounding marshland, the epitome of the unspoilt country town. With its cobbled streets and picturesque old buildings, including the Ypres Tower which dates from 1250, time seems to have stood still here.

The serenity of today belies a more traumatic past. It was battered by the sea in medieval times, losing its eastern quarter in the terrible storm of 1288, repeatedly mauled by French invaders, who practically destroyed the place in the raid of 1377, and heavily bombed during the Second World War.

Mermaid Street is the most celebrated part of Rye, tumbling down the steep hill from 'The Citadel' among timber-framed houses which include the famous Mermaid Inn, a magnet for holiday snappers and professional film makers alike, which was once a haunt of the notorious – and ruthless – Hawkhurst Gang of smugglers.

Artists and writers have been drawn to the town's charms down the years, including Henry James, Radclyffe Hall and E. F. Benson – who immortalised the place as Tilling (after the nearby River Tillingham) in his Mapp and Lucia books.

The church clock dates from 1561 and is one of the oldest in Britain to be working in its original position. Above it stand the

Celebrated Mermaid Street

golden quarterboys, so called because they strike only the quarter hours, with their quotation from the Apocrypha: 'For our time is a very shadow which passeth away.'

Until the end of the 16th century Rye was an important port and shipbuilding centre, when great merchant vessels from the ports of northern Europe tied up alongside a large fishing fleet at quaysides now two miles inland following the sea's retreat. Today only yachts and small pleasure craft can navigate the River Rother that flows peacefully below the town.

The peaceful River Rother below Rye

WINCHELSEA – THE SMALLEST TOWN IN ENGLAND

Below the down the stranded town
Hears far away the rollers beat;
About the wall the seabirds call;
The salt wind murmurs through the street;
Forlorn the sea's forsaken bride
Awaits the end that shall betide.
John Davidson, *A Cinque Port*

An attractive corner

While most towns are villages that grew, this place did the reverse with a history that has been singularly unlucky. It had its own Mint before the Conquest and by the 11th century was a port of considerable significance. But in 1250 it was partially submerged by the sea, and matters were not helped sixteen years later when Prince Edward sacked the place to put an end to the indiscriminate piracy that was rife among Winchelsea's seamen. Another great storm destroyed the old settlement in 1287.

A fresh start was made on a site further inland with a model new town which must have been the medieval planner's dream and was designed on the grid system. With its tidal harbour on the River Brede, Winchelsea became a member of the Cinque Ports Confederacy, providing ships for the country's defence. But repeated raids by the French (and the Spanish) devastated the place, the sea retreated, the harbour silted up and the once proud port was marooned.

There were 39 squares on the planners' grid at the end of the 13th century yet many were never built on and a mere dozen now exist. However, these are a source of delight for residents and visitors alike, with many fine houses, ancient gateways and the stone Court Hall, containing a small local museum which graphically shows how the coastline has changed over the centuries.

For all its misfortunes, Winchelsea can boast to be 'the smallest town in England' with a mayor and corporation elected with due pomp and ceremony every Easter Monday.

A tree marks the spot where John Wesley, the great apostle of the 18th century, preached his last open air sermon – 'that poor skeleton of ancient Winchelsea' he called it – and you can see the house where the actress Dame Ellen Terry lived.

Winchelsea was a major medieval port before the coastline changed

HASTINGS – A PROUD TOWN

Hastings arouses strong likes and dislikes. Personally, I think that on a fine day in late autumn when the holiday season is over, the Old Town is one of the pleasantest places on the South Coast.
Desmond Seward, *Sussex*

The classic Victorian seaside town, with a jumble of interesting architecture along the promenade, hides the much more historic Hastings.

Old Town rises towards the castle brooding high on the sandstone clifftop, built by the Normans to subdue the local populace after the Battle of Hastings in 1066 (actually fought six miles north-west of the town at Senlac Hill). Two ancient thoroughfares, High Street and All Saints Street, boast many timber-framed buildings and the raised pavement to be found in the former is itself a listed architectural feature.

This is a town with a proud maritime tradition. The harbour was silted up by the storms of 700 years ago, but Hastings has maintained its fishing fleet against all the odds. The fishermen pull their boats up along the eastern foreshore in an area known as The Stade and their tall black 'net shops', wooden buildings for storing nets and other equipment, have stood for centuries.

A question mark hangs over the future of the pier but the prom and beach is still a jaunty place to be on summer days.

The East Hill Lift, opened in 1903, is one of the steepest of its kind in England, with a gradient that is practically vertical (1/1.28). Until electrification in 1974, this was one of the last water balance cliff railways in the country, with water tanks holding 600

Hastings Pier

gallons. It saves a climb of 272 steps up the cliff to the glorious sea and rural views of the five-mile Hastings Country Park.

Against all the odds, Hastings fishermen continue a proud tradition

A PLACE OF BEAUTY AND OF BATTLE

See you yon stilly woods of oak, and the dread ditch beside?
Oh that was where the Saxons broke, on the day that Harold died
Rudyard Kipling

The Victorian writer Coventry Patmore had a liking for Sedlescombe, describing it as surpassing 'all other Sussex villages except Mayfield in its beautiful half-timbered houses of the XVI and XVIIIc. The chief inn of the place is a model of many gabled beauty and bad interior arrangement.'

Not much has changed since Patmore's day and the picturesque nature of the village is obviously a source of pride for residents as it has won a string of best-kept village and anti-litter awards down the years. These triumphs are recorded at the pillared well house on the village green, built in 1900 over the parish pump.

Battle Abbey was built on the site of the famous 1066 battlefield by William the Conqueror in thanksgiving for the victory that decided the fate of England. A plaque in the ruined church marks the spot where King Harold fell.

The Normans and the Saxons clashed at Senlac ('Sand Lake') Hill, an atmospheric place fringed by great trees, and Battle is a town which grew from this national disaster. At the Dissolution of the Monasteries the abbey was given to Sir Anthony Browne, who dismantled the church and quarried the building for stone. This in turn found its way to what is now Battle Abbey School next door and in other buildings along the pretty High Street – the Bell Inn did particularly well.

Another feature in this part of town is the arched spaces

Battle Abbey, where a Conqueror gave thanks

between many of the buildings, particularly on the south side. These were the entrances for carriages in days when there were coaching inns here in profusion. The coming of the railway put an end to that business.

The black monks of the Benedictine order inhabited the abbey for almost 500 years. The most impressive part of the remains – the great gatehouse with its towers, battlements and arrow slits – dates from the 14th century when permission to crenellate was given because of the threat of French attacks.

Picturesque Sedlescombe village

FAIRYTALE CASTLE COMMANDING THE ROTHER

The nearest the castle ever came to action was during the Wars of the Roses, in 1483, when the Lancastrians took it from the Yorkists, but apparently nobody was hurt.
Ben Darby, *Journey Through the Weald*

Bodiam's breathtaking castle

The fairytale Bodiam Castle is the gem of the rolling borderland with Kent. With its mighty, mellow towers reflected in the moat it appears almost to be floating on air. It was built at the end of the 14th century to protect the upper reaches of the River Rother from possible incursions by the French.

But the arrow slits, cannon ports and 'murder holes' (through which missiles could be dropped through the ceiling on attackers) were never used in anger. The castle fell into decay, was rescued in 1829 by 'Mad Jack' Fuller of Brightling when a Hastings builder planned to demolish it, and was then restored by two later owners, George Cubitt and Lord Curzon, who presented it to the nation. Under the care of the National Trust it is now a breathtaking if incongruous part of the landscape. The moat is fed by springs and the water is certainly purer now than in medieval times – there are no fewer than 28 garderobes or latrines at Bodiam, each with a drain shaft to the moat.

Bodiam commands the Rother Valley, stretching out below in a patchwork of water-meadows. The river is little more than a stream as it winds eastwards before descending to the sea and today it is hard to believe that in medieval times French warships could have travelled so far inland. In fact it was once navigable as far as Etchingham, where the Rother is joined by the Dudwell and the Limden. The vessels carried iron from Sir Robert Tyrrwhitt's forge in the village, and forges at Hurst Green and Robertsbridge, to the port of Rye.

There is no authentication of the widely held belief that the River Rother rises in the cellars of a house called Rotherhurst, a mile south of Rotherfield, but maps certainly show it rising in the grounds of the property.

Frost at dawn on the banks of the Rother

VILLAGE OF BEAUTY IN THE HIGH WEALD

When the Romans landed in Pevensey Bay, they had with them a dog called Bur, and after a while the dog got so bemired with the Sussex clay that he couldn't travel any further, so they washed him and the place where they washed him was called Burwash.
Old villager to the Rev John Coker Egerton, *Sussex Folk and Sussex Ways*

A spring morning in the High Weald and a view looking north from Burwash Common. This is a designated Area of Outstanding Natural Beauty, and it is easy to see why. The road eastwards from Heathfield runs along a ridge offering awe-inspiring views on either side and passes through two 'Burwashes', Common and Weald, before reaching the place itself.

The village so beloved of the writer Rudyard Kipling is renowned for its picturesque qualities; a long main street with a feast of old houses, some tile hung, some weatherboarded, and screened by a row of pollarded limes on the north side. Many of them have been there from medieval times but the prize for venerability goes to Chateaubriand which has the remains of a quasi-aisle dating from the 13th century.

The largest and most opulent in appearance of all the 'gentlemen's residences' in the High Street is Rampyndene which dates from 1699 – and has bizarre associations. When Captain John Leyland Feilden's wife died in 1887 he refused to communicate with the rector, with whom he had fallen out. Instead he had her body embalmed and put in a small mausoleum in the garden. The captain left the remains of his wife behind when he moved to the West Country and it was left to his

The Bell Inn at Burwash

brother, Arctic explorer Henry Wemyss Feilden, to have them removed and buried in the churchyard.

The Bell Inn, opposite the church, is the height of respectability today but it has a shadier past. It was once the haunt of smugglers who made use of the close proximity of St Bartholomew's to hide contraband in the tombs of the churchyard. The inn also welcomed parishioners in need of refreshment after church vestry meetings.

The view from Burwash Common

BATEMANS – JUST AS KIPLING LEFT IT

The study . . . seems eternally to await his return, with all his books on the shelves, the Indian rugs especially woven for him, his huge wastepaper basket and the desk littered with his accumulated writer's paraphernalia of paperweight, pen tray, ruler and the like.
David Arscott, _The County in Colour_

Rudyard Kipling, 'The Writer of Empire', is so firmly associated with India that it seems hard to believe he visited the sub-continent for the final time at the age of 25.

The rose garden

If India was his first love, Sussex was most definitely his second. He lived firstly at Rottingdean and then, to escape the intrusive attentions of his admiring public, at Batemans in Burwash, built for a 17th century ironmaster. It remained his home from 1902 until his death 34 years later.

The measure of his delight at discovering this fine old house is conveyed in his autobiography _Something of Myself_ where he describes the first sight of Batemans from the driving seat of his Locomobile steam car. 'We had seen an advertisement for her, and we reached her down an enlarged rabbit warren of a lane. At first sight the Committee of Ways and Means said: "That's her! The only she! Make an honest woman of her – quick!"'

The Kiplings lavished much time and thought on the gardens of the house. His wife Caroline designed the rose garden and pond and planted the yew hedges that border them to this day. He adapted the watermill to generate electricity but 'as the little weir which turned her current into the little mill race was of frail antiquity, one had to attend to her often and at once, and always at the most inconvenient moments.'

Kipling drew inspiration from his environment, most noticeably in _Puck of Pook's Hill_, which stands above Batemans. He died in 1936 and his widow left the house to the nation in her will. Now administered by the National Trust, the study where Kipling wrote so many of his Sussex stories is as he left it, as are the other rooms that can be visited. The keen early motorist who discovered his gem at the bottom of the warren that day left one of his gleaming Rolls Royces for the public to view in his garage.

Rudyard Kipling fell in love with Batemans at first sight

THE CHARMS OF BEWL WATER

'Ill met by moonlight, proud Titania.'
William Shakespeare, *A Midsummer Night's Dream*

High summer at Bewl Water, a paradise for anglers, water sports enthusiasts, birdwatchers, walkers and Shakespeare lovers.

It has taken barely a quarter of a century for this entirely man-made reservoir to become a seamless part of the landscape. It covers 770 acres, has a capacity of 6,900 million gallons and is the largest expanse of water in south-east England. The whole of Bewl Water is now in East Sussex but only since a change of boundaries. When it was built between 1973 and 1975 in order to provide water for the Medway towns the main entrance was then in Kent.

Areas are now given over to fishing, sailing, rowing and even scuba diving and a nature reserve occupies more than 100 acres of the reservoir's central arm. In high summer it has become a popular and idyllic spot for theatrical performances – who could resist the Bard under the stars at the water's edge? – and for spectacular fireworks displays doubled in their intensity by the lake's reflection.

Winter, too, has its charms when the lure of water and woodland draws the hardier walkers. Here is a refuge for birds escaping the frozen conditions of northern and central Europe, and at Bewl can be found Brent and white-fronted geese, Bewick swans, waders and various species of duck.

Bewl was created when a tributary of the River Medway was dammed and the valley to the north of Ticehurst flooded. Dunster Mill House would have been totally submerged had not

Fishermen make full use of Bewl Water

its owner, Hubert Beale, successfully petitioned Parliament for its preservation. The Southern Water Authority paid for the 15th century house to be dismantled brick by brick and rebuilt some 500 yards away above the waterline. The machinery of Dunster watermill was also saved from submersion and re-sited with the house.

Bewl Water in winter

ENCHANTED BAYHAM ABBEY

O, Sussex is enchanted land! It lies within the heart
Although the lover and his love have long since dwelt apart.
Vera Arlett, *An Old Land*

Here's a beautiful winter mixture. Two arresting buildings, one lying in Sussex and the other in Kent. The people of the former are fortunate indeed to claim Bayham Abbey as their own, for there can surely be no prettier monastic ruins in the south-east. It has been compared with the examples to be found in Yorkshire.

The county border is formed by the Teise stream, a tributary of the Medway, which stands behind Bayham. Rising above it is the more modern Bayham Abbey, which is Kent's treasure. The Premonstratensian abbey dates from the 13th century, founded by Robert de Turneham and Ela de Sackville, and a considerable amount of the church and its surrounding buildings still remains. The north transept is not only standing but roofed, and the details of the carving on the capitals are particularly fine.

Not surprisingly the canons and their servants were reluctant to leave this slightly magical place. When the abbey was closed down by Cardinal Wolsey in 1525 they staged an armed sit-in which led to the arrest and imprisonment of the ringleaders. They were a tough bunch – the Premonstratensian Order was a strict one, whose mother abbey was at Premonstre, in Aisne.

Like most of the border country with Kent, the scenery in these parts can be stunning. The ruins of Bayham, standing in perfect peace as if rooted to the landscape, so deeply impressed Richard Church that he said in his book *Kent* (he was viewing

An autumn evening near Bayham

from the other side of the Teise) that he found it difficult to write about it, adding simply: 'It's beauty is so absolute.'

The ruins of Bayham Abbey

CAPTIVATING CASTLE AND TRADITIONAL TRUGS

You cannot comprehend Herstmonceux Castle in a day, neither can you do so in a week, nor in a month. I defy you to understand it in a year . . .
Arthur Beckett, *The Wonderful Weald*

A spring morning in Herstmonceux and the moated castle positively glows, russet red in the sunshine. For many years the home of the Royal Greenwich Observatory, it was built in 1441 by Sir Roger Fiennes – one of the earliest important brick buildings in the country, following the fashion that was made popular in Flanders. It is likely that the bricks were made by Flemish workmen specially imported for the job.

Sir Roger's descendant Thomas, Lord Dacre, received Anne of Cleves on her arrival in England in 1540 but, 'being a right towardly gentleman', was executed on Tower Hill at the age of 23, ostensibly for having caused the death of a gamekeeper while poaching with friends at Pikehay. More probably it was because of 'his great estate which greedy courtiers gaped after, causing them to hasten his destruction.'

The castle was later superseded by nearby Herstmonceux Place and had become ruinous until restoration in 1929 by Colonel Claude Lowther, who had raised three battalions in the Great War known as Lowther's Lambs. The task was completed in the 1930s by Sir Paul Catham.

Herstmonceux is the home of the trug, the oval shaped wooden basket that is a Jack-of-all-trades in the garden and home. Trug making is a traditional craft that has been established in Sussex for some 250 years but was first brought to the attention

Reg, Sussex trug maker

of a wider audience by Thomas Smith of Herstmonceux, who displayed his wares at the Great Exhibition of 1851. Queen Victoria showed such an interest that she ordered several trugs in various sizes which were delivered in person at Buckingham Palace by the enterprising Mr Smith, who travelled all the way there and back on foot.

Across the moat to Herstmonceux

THE WHISPERING MARSHES

If Bonyparte should have the heart, to land on Pemsey Level,
Then my three sons with their three guns, would blow him to the
devil
Local saying

Sunset on the Levels

If you seek solitude and atmosphere, Pevensey Levels is the place to find them. Great skies loom over countless flat but far from featureless acres and the breeze whispers constantly through the reeds.

These marshes, once completely under water, have for centuries been drained by a network of dykes. With modern, efficient pump drainage threatening to dry out the land to the detriment of its rich and diverse wildlife, English Nature bought 150 acres of undrained fields at Pevensey Bridge Level in the 1980s and entered into agreements with neighbouring landowners to prevent further drainage there. Similarly, when the Sussex Wildlife Trust increased its landholding here to more than 300 acres, it immediately set about introducing a network of new sluices in order to keep the pasture damp in the spring when breeding waders and wildfowl need to be able to probe for food.

So the Levels are a world of wet – a primitive environment recognised by ecologists as one of the finest in the world. Along the ditches and across the sodden pastures you will find as many as 120 rare insect species and around 70 per cent of the country's aquatic plants. This is one of only two British sites for our largest spider – the harmless fen raft spider, which can be found in practically every ditch. More than 20 species of dragonfly have been recorded here and these marshes are an important site for aquatic molluscs and blood-sucking leeches, which live down in the slime and feast upon frogs and fish.

Where the Levels meet the sea were erected the Martello Towers, 40 feet high and of such a thickness they required 50,000 bricks to complete a single course, to withstand the threatened Napoleonic invasion of England.

Pevensey Levels form one of the finest ecological environments in the world

A SACRED CIRCLE

Let the dark cypress tell my destiny,
And the green ivy form my funeral pall
Gideon Mantell, *Stanzas,* 1827

The heart of Hellingly is a charming array of old cottages around the oval shaped churchyard which rises seven feet in some places above the roads which surround it. It is the only 'ciric' or Celtic burial ground in Sussex to be preserved intact. The dead were lain in raised circular mounds because they were dry and because the circle was the old pagan symbol of immortality.

So they made it, so it remained. Nearby dwellings aged, decayed and tumbled down, to be replaced by new and different kinds of homes, but always the sacred circle was left untouched.

Nearby is Michelham Priory, seen across the placid moat from the south with the east wing of the original 13th century priory on the right. Most of the ecclesiastical buildings were razed to the foundations after the Dissolution of the Monasteries but parts of the remaining walls were later incorporated in the Tudor house that can be savoured today, more a mellow manor than a priory after the King's wreckers had finished with it.

The beautiful pale sandstone house stands within seven moated acres, formed by draining the River Cuckmere. The site was in use before the canons took it over; excavations have revealed what is thought to be part of a Norman manor house. The island may originally have been a Saxon clearing in the forest, 'michel ham' or 'micel ham' meaning a large clearing.

Two spectacular buildings of the original priory cluster remain. The first is the gatehouse tower, 60 feet tall with no other

Michelham Priory from the south

structure in the neighbourhood approaching its height, with its original stone walls. Secondly there is the great barn, whose 14th century bulk was increased 200 years later. The magnificent oak and elm timbers inside are mostly the medieval originals.

Hellingly's old cottages

MOST ELEGANT OF SEASIDE RESORTS

. . . an ecstasy of building of such taste and quality that Eastbourne became known as the 'Empress of Watering Places' in the 1880s.
Peter Brandon, *The Sussex Landscape*

The South Downs end (or begin, depending on your viewpoint) where they tumble down to the sea at Eastbourne.

This most elegant of seaside resorts was envisaged as 'a town built by gentlemen for gentlemen.' There was next to nothing here in the middle of the 19th century and no hint of the grandeur to come – the 'old town' which was no more than a village and, on the coast itself, a handful of fishermen's cottages. All that changed in 1858 when the Earl of Burlington, who owned almost two thirds of the area, became the Seventh Duke of Devonshire and, overnight, one of the wealthiest men in England. With Carew Davies Gilbert, one time President of the Royal Society who owned about a quarter of the surrounding countryside, he set about creating a town of broad leafy avenues, parks and generous villas. Even today, the town retains a great deal of its original spaciousness.

Covenants ensure that the seafront is not commercialised, and the gardens west of the pier are among the great attractions for visitors. They come in their thousands every summer, a genteel bunch for the most part because Eastbourne is a class apart from the more happy-go-lucky 'candy floss and whelks' seaside resorts, even though it has a pier with amusement arcades built in 1872 by Eugenius Birch, who was also responsible for Brighton's West Pier.

Here in 'The Suntrap of the South' holidaymakers can enjoy gentler amusements which include band concerts and tea dances.

The composer Claude Debussy was here in 1905 in search of solace after the breakdown of his first marriage. Eastbourne must have fallen short of his expectations for he described it sourly as: 'A little seaside town, silly as these places sometimes are' and with 'too many draughts and too much music.'

Looking towards the pier

Eastbourne from the Downs

BEACHY HEAD – THE BEAUTIFUL HEADLAND

The impassable precipice shuts off our former selves of yesterday, forcing us to look out over the sea only, or up to the deeper heaven.
Richard Jefferies, *The Breeze on Beachy Head*

It's wild, beautiful and strangely sad, this range of white cliffs with the hulking monster at its centre. At 534 feet, Beachy Head is the highest point on the south coast, with an unhappy record of suicide attempts – most of them successful.

On a happier note, many a sailor's life has been saved by the light that shines for 25 miles out to sea from the lighthouse at the foot of the cliffs. As long ago as 1670 there was a light at the summit, made more sophisticated in 1828 when James Walker built a 47 foot high circular stone tower. Though often obscured by fog or low cloud while the air below was quite clear, it continued in use until 1899 when it was decided that a new lighthouse was needed – particularly as the weight of the existing one was likely to cause the cliff to collapse at any moment.

The present tower, built in the sea and a minor miracle of construction for its time, is 142 feet high and the flashing light is 103 feet above the level of mean high water. In fog, an electrically powered signal sounds every 30 seconds.

The name Beachy Head is derived from the French *beau chef*, or beautiful headland, though the many shipwrecks which have occurred here down the centuries explain why Venetian sailors once called it 'The Devil's Cape'.

To stand on the edge of this sheer drop – there are no fences to protect you from the edge of the Downs and the sea – is calculated to make a mountain goat feel giddy and not

The present lighthouse

recommended for those with the slightest trace of vertigo. The sea boils below, the clouds fly above and somewhere between the two the gulls scream madly.

A scene of wild beauty at Beachy Head

A LIVING PICTURE OF OLD ENGLAND

But here the Old Gods guard their round,
And, in her secret heart,
The heathen kingdom Wilfrid found
Dreams, as she dwells, apart.
Rudyard Kipling, *Sussex*

Wood anemones cover the ground

The loneliest place in the county; and one of the loveliest. Even people who profess to have a knowledge of Sussex have never heard of it. In loneliness lies beauty. Penhurst is a church, a manor house and a few farm buildings, a living picture of old England that has scarcely changed since Shakespeare's day. The hairpin bends that shield it from the rest of the world are calculated to cut it off completely during the ice and snow of winter.

As the writer Barbara Willard put it: 'This is the intensest countryside for miles – turned in upon itself, separate, pinned to the past, silent, undisturbed, as country should be.'

In the Elizabethan manor house are the last three firebacks cast at the last furnace of the Sussex iron industry at neighbouring Ashburnham. The name of the man who did the job before the fire was extinguished for good in 1813 has been recorded for posterity. He was Will Rummins, according to a former rector of Penhurst, the Rev R. W. Whistler, who was given the name by the last surviving labourer at Ashburnham Furnace, William Hobday, who died in August 1883.

A little ingenuity keeps the congregation of the church comfortable in the winter when hot air is pumped into the old building by an agricultural corn drier. The old copper lamp at the entrance to the churchyard strikes an even more incongruous note – it once lit the streets of Clerkenwell in London.

Surrounded by dense woods, a joy in springtime when anemones scatter the ground like jewels, Penhurst keeps her secrets. The 21st century is left far behind and it is easy to believe the legend that in the sinister-sounding Creep Wood the Britons made a last stand in a desperate battle against the Saxons.

Penhurst has hardly changed through the centuries

THE LIGHTHOUSE THAT MOVED

When from the sea with wide-spread wings,
The Mist rolls o'er the Downs;
It fills the vale, the beacon height
With mantle dank it crowns
Frederick Harrison, *When the Mist Rolls o'er the Downs*

In a book concerned with the East Sussex landscape, Belle Tout is one of the most up-to-date features – it only came to be on its site in 1999! How can that be when the former lighthouse dates from 1828, a splendid piece of Georgian architecture that combines functionality with elegance?

The old lighthouse was in a precarious position on its lofty clifftop perch near Beachy Head. The chalk was eroding from the edge so rapidly that there was a real danger that the old building would tumble into the sea. So the owners of one of the more spectacular homes in the county had it moved back inland to safety – an event which attracted international attention and brought the world's media to the south coast in droves. With ingenious use of hydraulics and rails, millimetre by painstaking millimetre it was dragged away from the cliff edge to a new site some 50 metres away. It was a feat of engineering and planning that resulted in just one single, insignificant crack appearing on an internal wall.

Belle Tout served the Channel's mariners well throughout Queen Victoria's reign but was replaced by the present candy striped lighthouse because her warning beams of light at the top of the cliffs were often obscured by fog or low cloud.

Belle Tout was always one of the most romantic of seaside

Removed to safety

structures, however, and a favourite with artists. The building even took a starring role in the TV drama *The Life and Loves of a She-Devil*.

Belle Tout lighthouse is one of the most spectacular homes in Sussex

CLASSIC SUSSEX VILLAGES

I shall build me a house of high thatch,
Within a walk of the sea,
And the men who were boys when I was a boy,
Shall sit and drink with me.
Hilaire Belloc, *The South Country*

Here is a classic English village, with its picturesque grouping of flint cottages around the green. Add to that its proximity to the sea at Birling Gap and you can understand why East Dean is a

Awaiting the next collection at West Dean

sought-after place to live. The pride in the place shines through in this home of green-fingered expertise.

The Tiger Inn, eye-catcher of the oldest part of the community, probably got its name by error. It was taken from the Bardolf coat of arms which depicts a leopard. This would have been an understandable mistake 400 years ago when a simple innkeeper would never have seen either beast.

The Bardolf family lived at Birling Manor and had the unhappy knack of backing the wrong side. Hugh Bardolf was adviser to the ill-fated King John and Lord Thomas Bardolf (who appears in Shakespeare's *Henry IV*) took part in the Earl of Northumberland's revolt against Henry IV, was wounded in battle and died soon afterwards. In 1406 he was posthumously dishonoured in Parliament and his lands forfeited to the Crown. Birling was later granted back to the family, only to be finally lost in 1461 because Lord William Bardolf fought for the Lancastrians against Edward IV.

At West Dean, a delightful conservation village with mosaic-like flint walls buried away deep inside Friston Forest, can be found what is maintained to be the oldest inhabited rectory in the country, dating in part from 1220 with walls two and half feet thick and a stone spiral staircase.

Boasting such a venerable building, it is possible to believe that Alfred the Great had his palace at West Dean. Certainly Asser, the monk who was to become a bishop and the King's biographer, was summoned to visit Alfred here and recorded his royal welcome.

East Dean's lovely cottages

THE MYSTERIOUS GIANT

I will go out against the sun
Where the rolled scarp retires,
And the Long Man of Wilmington
Looks naked towards the shires . . .
Rudyard Kipling, *Sussex*

The Long Man of Wilmington towers above the village on Windover Hill. This faceless outline of a man carved into the chalk, standing some 230 feet high with two staves in his hands slightly longer than himself, still remains a mystery.

Was he created by the monks at the priory? Is he of Roman origin? Or do his roots lie in the Neolithic period? Perhaps the staves are divining rods, perhaps the parts of a door whose lintel has eroded away.

There are many theories about his identity, from a giant killed on this spot by a hammer thrown by another at Firle, to an ancient god throwing open the gates of dawn. He may look 'naked towards the shires', as Kipling wrote, but he lacks the most celebrated attribute of the Cerne Abbas giant in Dorset – despite periodic attempts to remedy the situation. The offending additions to his anatomy have been hastily removed.

His outline now preserved in white concrete blocks (replacing the yellow bricks installed in 1873), the Long Man can proudly lay claim to being one of the largest representations of the human form in the world. The earliest evidence yet discovered as to his age is an early 18th century illustration at Chatsworth House in Derbyshire.

His creators seem to have had a good idea of perspective

The giant's friendly neighbours

because he is abnormally tall when seen close up but perfectly proportioned from a distance. Whether he has stood here thousands of years or barely three hundred, the Long Man is giving nothing away as he towers serenely above the Weald with the seasons ever changing below him.

The Long Man of Wilmington – but who was he?

A RARE AND ANCIENT MARKET CROSS

*The Downsman looks on the plain below, where among a
thousand trees
A hundred grey-green villages lie dozing upon the leas.*
Arthur Beckett, *The Spirit of the Downs*

The delights of Alfriston are so numerous that it is little wonder
the village is overrun with tourists during the summer months.
They are drawn by its timber-framed houses, venerable inns and
tea rooms; by a church steeped in legend, wondrous views and the
first building ever purchased by the National Trust.

Miraculously Afriston remains unspoiled, a gem of a place
nestling in the valley where the Downs give way to the River
Cuckmere. It seems to remain serene and aloof amid all the bustle
and tripper traffic, and, when dusk falls and the visitors have all
gone home, adopts the slightly secretive air it had for the
centuries before the invention of motorised transport.

The ancient market cross stands at the head of the long
High Street in Waterloo Square – a name adopted during the
Napoleonic Wars when the village was garrisoned by troops. The
cross is one of only two in Sussex, the other being at Chichester,
and was probably first built in 1405 when Henry IV granted
Alfriston the right to hold a weekly market. It was partly
demolished by a lorry in 1955.

Nearby is The Smugglers, an inn with six staircases, 21
rooms and no fewer than 47 doors – perfect for hiding things and
for making quick getaways, and a relic of the days when the area
was a hotbed of smuggling.

St Andrew's church, famed 'cathedral of the Downs', stands

The Clergy House

beside the village green known as The Tye. It was here that the
custom persisted of placing a wreath of white flowers upon the
coffins of virgins and afterwards hanging the garlands in the
church for the following twelve months.

In the shadow of the church is the 14th century Clergy
House, bought by the National Trust in 1896 for the princely sum
of £10.

Alfriston's medieval market cross, one of only two in Sussex

THROUGH THE CUCKMERE VALLEY

*I walked the hills and valleys
And tasted all the summer's pride*
William Blake, *Songs of Innocence*

This is the visitor centre of the Seven Sisters Country Park at Exceat – where you are assured of a spectacular welcome. Here are the Meanders of the River Cuckmere in all their glory, making their way to the sea from the lush water meadows of 'Millionaire's Valley' to the north and south from Exceat in slow, graceful curves.

The Cuckmere's sinuous progress begins some twenty miles inland among the wooded ridges astride Heathfield and continues amid a thick embroidery of reeds and rushes and willow herb through the green patchwork of the low Weald. No more than a brook until now, it suddenly widens below the A27 for the last dramatic miles to the sea past villages of flint and thatch.

It was in 1977 that East Sussex County Council acquired the Seven Sisters Country Park – nearly 700 acres of the Cuckmere Valley and its adjoining coastline – and set about conserving its scenic beauty to give people the chance to explore and enjoy it. Cars are banned and only sheep are allowed to graze here in order to maintain the grassland in the traditional manner. The visitor centre is at a converted 18th century barn, where displays explain the history, geography and wildlife of the area.

Exploring the valley by air!

The Seven Sisters Country Park

THE BEACH AT BIRLING GAP

And north Sussex is always looking south, to the Downs which become a firmer guarantee of the sea beyond than an uninterrupted view could have been.
Ian Nairn, *The Buildings of England – Sussex*

The waves hammer in towards the white walls of Birling Gap, the rim of England where the South Downs end abruptly and the Channel begins. It's a spectacular landscape that's constantly in a state of flux with clifftop erosion gnawing away between two and three feet a year.

It has had a particular effect here at the Gap where a Victorian coastguard cottage has been lost and others are in a precarious position. The nearby pub is in jeopardy, too, with the cliff edge drawing ever closer. You can access the beach from here down a series of steps set against the cliff edge and crunch along the shoreline. Keeping a sharp eye out for the tides, it is possible to walk from Seaford to Eastbourne along this rocky road of the foreshore. Not only is this one of the longest stretches of undeveloped coastline in the south east, but since 1987 it has been declared a conservation area, giving it protection 2,000 metres out to sea.

It's a dazzling experience on a clear day, literally, with the sun beating off the twin mirrors of the sea and the white cliffs.

A secret marine world exists out there beneath the waves in the deep gullies of the extensive chalk reef; it can be glimpsed when the sea recedes leaving weedy rock pools teeming with crabs, fish, limpets and anemones.

It is possible to walk from Seaford to Eastbourne

The naturalist Richard Jefferies recorded a trip to the Gap in *The Breeze on Beachy Head*. 'Upon the beach lies a piece of timber, part of a wreck; the wood is torn and the fibres rent where it was battered against the dull edge of the rocks. The heat of the sun burns, thrown back by the dazzling chalk; the river of ocean flows ceaselessly, casting the spray over the stones; the unchanged sky is blue.'

Sunset over the sea at Birling Gap

SEVEN SISTERS AND SHEPHERDS' CROWNS

'Those sturdy girls who hand in hand, and hand in hand,
paddle at the water's edge.'
Capt George Victor Osborne Taylor, *Darling Kate*
(letters from France)

The sheer face of the cliffs

Here's one of Britain's most instantly recognisable and much-loved images: the emerald and white humps of The Seven Sisters cliffs, with the Cuckmere Haven coastguard cottages in the foreground. If the view is familiar, the names of the 'sisters', stretching from the Haven to Birling Gap, probably are not. They are christened Haven Brow, Short Brow, Rough Brow, Brass Point, Flagstaff Point, Bailey's Brow and Went Hill Brow. The arcs of chalk, soaring up to 260 feet in height, probably got their collective name from Elizabethan mariners.

Draw a straight line south from the face of The Seven Sisters and try to find land. What do you hit first? France? No, the West Indies. Undercut and battered by waves, split by frost, the Sisters are shrinking back from the sea and the gaps between them are widening. Thousands of years from now they will completely divide to form separate headlands.

This is one of the few sites in Britain where you can find the red star thistle, its seeds perhaps originally carried to England by soldiers returning from the Napoleonic Wars. Here, too, you can comb the beach for fossilised sea urchins, known as shepherds' crowns and highly prized by country folk who keep them for good luck.

The chalk 'shelf' of the shoreline covers the area between high and low tide marks and is ideal for molluscs like winkles, whelks and limpets, and for crustaceans such as crabs, prawns and barnacles. This makes it an ideal feeding ground for seabirds. In the deeper gullies swim fish with strange names like Goldsinny and Ballan Wrasse.

With so much of the Sussex coast under tarmac and concrete, this majestic stretch of cliffs is protected by its country park status for future generations to come and enjoy open downland with spectacular coastal views. Here is a haven for everything from butterflies to badgers, and the crickets chirrup through the warmth of the day.

The Seven Sisters cliffs

WINDING LONELY TO THE SEA

And as you sit upon the cliff and sniff the salty sea,
You'll see a lugger standing in, men wading to the knee.
Arthur Beckett, *Downland*

A winter's day at Cuckmere Haven, where the river makes its lazy, winding entrance and union with the sea between Seaford Head and The Seven Sisters. It's the most unspoilt river mouth in the county, with none of the usual man-made intrusions; no harbour, no railway, no housing development. The only interference with this supremely natural spot occurred in 1846 when the Cuckmere's progress to the sea was bypassed by a cut to combat persistent shingle drift and the river was embanked to lessen flooding in the valley.

Known locally as the Meanders, the river twists and turns as if reluctant to leave Sussex. On higher ground close by once stood the fishing village of Exceat, the target of repeated raids by the French which led to it finally being abandoned in the 15th century. All that remains is a tablet erected on the site of the 13th century church by the Sussex Archaeological Society.

It's about a mile downstream from the road to the beach, enough to deter a large percentage of motorised trippers, so even in high summer Cuckmere Haven will be relatively empty. Those seeking total seclusion should come in the winter when the chances are there will be no human company at all. Remote and atmospheric, it particularly appeals to ornithologists.

A little inland there's a park trail for walkers, a marked circuit for horse riders and a small camp site. Fishing, rowing and canoeing are catered for, too.

The Meanders

At the mouth of the river a path climbs steeply to the west past the picturesque old coastguard cottages to the nature reserve on Seaford Head; to the east the South Downs Way continues its switchback course across The Seven Sisters towards the mighty wall of Beachy Head.

Cuckmere Haven is a place of total seclusion in winter

OF GRASS AND SKY

Oh, we are king and queen today,
Of this good green land that clouds sail over,
The valleys abrim with lilac and may,
The spaces of unsearched grass and clover.
Arthur Bell, *On Bury Combe*

They run from Eastbourne in the east to Winchester in the west, a spectacular line of hills, 'a kingdom of grass and sky', that have inspired in some an awesome adoration.

The South Downs, steep and shady on the northern escarpment, gentle and sun-kissed to the south where the breezes come in from the sea.

Arthur Beckett, in *The Spirit of the Downs*, was moved to write: 'The Downland air is always fresh and pure. It has a quality which elevates the spirits and braces the physical frame.' And he bounds with a great shout across the springy turf to receive from the Spirit of his book's title 'the gift that makes a man master of the world.'

The curate naturalist Gilbert White granted them an unusual status when he wrote of 'a chain of majestic mountains'; Edward Thomas said 'the highest points command much of earth, all of heaven'; and Rudyard Kipling lavished the most praise of all: '. . . our close-bit thyme that smells like dawn in Paradise.'

Other herbs such as basil and marjoram add their delicate fragrances, and the springy turf is studded with colourful violets, harebells, cowslips (if you're lucky) and orchids.

Rare cowslips

Sheep have been reintroduced in some areas by conservationists in order to preserve the precious wildlife habitat produced by their constant cropping of grasses and shrubs which would otherwise be all-smothering.

The South Downs Way, some 80 miles of it, follows an ancient route along the ridge with the sea on one side and the Weald fading from green to grey to blue on the other. From Ditchling Beacon, the highest point in East Sussex, you can see the distant North Downs which follow a roughly parallel course through Surrey and Kent.

Below the Downs, like a little chain of jewels along their length, are the ancient settlements of Sussex, flint cottages, Norman churches and grand houses.

The flower-sprinkled turf of the Downs

THE SOUTH DOWNS AT FIRLE

Beneath that breadth of sky, God's hand had wrought
With pattern cloud, and in that air like leaven
Nothing could live but lofty aim, pure thought,
Elated peace, and hope as high as heaven.
Daniel Coombes, *The High Ground*

Changing seasons looking west towards Firle Beacon, a view particularly popular with artists – the fresh green of spring and the parched panorama of an August harvest.

Kipling writes of 'our blunt, bow-headed, whale-backed downs', while other writers have seen more feminine shapes in these rounded hills – perhaps the most extreme but poetic being Anthony Armstrong, in *The Year At Margarets*, who described 'Those green curves as soft and gentle as the breasts of a sleeping girl.'

Firle Beacon, 718 feet in height, formed part of the great chain of high points on which fires were lit to warn of national emergency, notably the approach of the Spanish Armada. It also gave the weather forecast for the folk in the neighbouring village of Alciston, pronounced A'ston in the old days:

When Firle and Long Man wear a cap,
We at A'ston gets a drap.

Firle itself (properly West Firle, though you won't find a north, south or east) is a classic downland community built in the sheltered shadow of the hills, a charming cluster of houses and cottages in a single street leading to the church.

Much of the village is the estate of Firle Place, home of the

The fresh green curves of the Downs

Gage family since the 15th century. The big house was substantially altered in around 1730, though some signs of the earlier building can still be seen, and houses a number of notable Old Masters, some fine French and English furniture and a famous collection of Sevres porcelain.

The greengage was first grown in England at Firle Place, introduced by the botanical traveller Thomas Gage, and another Thomas was Commander in Chief of the British forces in America at the outbreak of the American War of Independence. In June 1775, he fought and lost the Battle of Bunker Hill and resigned.

Looking across the Downs to Firle Beacon on a ripe August day

The Sussex men that dwell upon the shore
Look out when storms arise and billows roar
Devoutly praying with uplifted hands
That some well-laden ships may skim the sands
To which whose rich cargo they may make pretence
And fatten on the spoils of providence.
Arthur Congreve, *The Spoils*

The gleaming white eminence of Seaford Head dominates the town. Never quite a resort – despite great and embryonic plans for its development in the early 19th century – Seaford can justifiably claim to be the only 'seaside town' in East Sussex.

Seaford has a long history and a singularly unlucky one. In medieval times it stood at the mouth of the River Ouse and was a port and ship-building centre of great importance, becoming a member of the Cinque Ports Confederation. But nature and man contrived to rob the place of its lifeblood.

By tradition, a violent storm in 1565 diverted the Ouse mouth from Seaford to neighbouring Meeching ('new haven'). Such an overnight disaster seems unlikely and though the storm may have played a part in making up minds there is evidence that the diversion of the river was a deliberate act to improve its navigation. This involved making a cut directly to the sea at the present site of Newhaven harbour.

It left Seaford in a state of living death and its fortunes did not revive until the arrival of the first seaside patrons towards the end of the 18th century.

The Martello Tower on the seafront now houses the

The Martello Tower

Seaford local history museum, with an emphasis on ships and shipwrecks for which the bay was infamous. It was a prolonged attack on a squat round tower at Mortella Point, Corsica, during the Napoleonic Wars in 1794 which gave the British Army the idea of constructing a chain of 74 similar sturdy defences along the south coast against possible French invasion. Seaford's is the most westerly of them and nobody seems to have noticed, or cared, that they got the name wrong.

Looking west over the town from the summit of Seaford Head

NEWHAVEN – A BUSY LITTLE HARBOUR

'Here's a grubbly little place; a noisy little place of fish smells and river smells and cheap tobacco. When it's over we must come here on vacation.'
Canadian soldier, World War Two

The harbour

Sussex has two harbours (the other being at Shoreham) and Newhaven is undoubtedly the more colourful. It's the only port between Dover and Portsmouth which is accessible at all states of the tides for vessels of up to four metres draft. The deep inlet of the River Ouse is alive with cross-Channel ferries, fishing boats, cargo boats, yachts and pleasure craft.

Not exactly beautiful, but certainly bustling, the port has a history dating back to 1736 when parliamentary powers were first granted for its development and work started on enlarging the harbour, building a pier and deepening the channel. Regular dredging is necessary to maintain its depth.

This vibrant mouth of the Ouse is dominated by Newhaven Fort, which never fired a shot in anger but is some measure of how strategically important the town was. Now a major tourist attraction, the fort was commissioned by Lord Palmerston in the 1860s to counter a hostile threat (which never materialised) from the French. Built into the chalk hill, it features gun emplacements, mortar batteries, magazines and a labyrinth of underground passages.

The fort had an important coastal defence role during both world wars and was the main base for the disastrous raid on Dieppe in 1942 — there is a memorial at the junction of Bridge Street and the ring road, to the many Canadian soldiers who died — and, two years later, it was one of the assembly points for vessels and troops involved in the D-Day landings.

A small army unit continued to occupy the fort until 1962, after which the buildings were allowed to decay and became a source of wood and building materials for all. In 1979 the fort was scheduled as an ancient monument and restoration work began in 1981. 'Palmerston's Folly' now houses a fascinating range of exhibits.

Newhaven Fort overlooks the bustling harbour

TELSCOMBE, THE TIMELESS HAMLET

And the vision fading slowly
In the golden evening air,
Seemed to have a Soul that whispered
All things peaceful, all things fair.
H. M. Walbrook

Tiny Telscombe is like a well-kept secret – a delight to discover. As David Hardman wrote in a book of praise to a place with barely forty inhabitants: 'One comes upon it from the Newhaven side or from the valley of the Ouse, or after stumbling over the rough track from Subtopia, with dramatic suddenness. The steep coombe and the village in it are quite unexpected. It has an unreality, like a memory of some rural etching in a Victorian album. Here, within a very few miles of the cosmopolitan bustle of Brighton, is the warmth of secluded homesteads sheltered by the shapely humps and folds of the Downs.'

The unlovely coastal development sprawls across the cliffs less than a mile away, but here is a perfect piece of old England. Untouched and unspoiled. There is only one way in for car travellers and the narrow lane peters out at a spot famous for its bank of wild daffodils in springtime. A church dating back to Saxon times, a cluster of old cottages and the majestic, primitive changelessness of empty hills all around . . . this remote place is certainly idyllic and owes its character to one man.

Retired bookmaker, Ambrose Gorham, became squire and benefactor of Telscombe at the end of the 19th century. He refused to allow any development to take place there but was not a backward-thinking patriarch. He improved the state of the cottages, restored the Church of St Lawrence and brought

The South Downs near Telscombe

electricity into the village in 1930. When he died in 1933, the squire bequeathed all his land to Brighton Corporation in trust, stating in his will that the purpose of the gift was to preserve the rural nature of the village.

Telscombe

FLAMBOYANCE AND FUN

If you approve of flirtations, good dinners,
Seascapes divine which the merry winds whiten,
Nice little saints and still nicer young sinners –
Winter in Brighton!
Mortimer Collins, *Winter in Brighton*

'London by the sea' . . . a heady mixture of the grand and the seedy; the flamboyant and the fun. Since the first train steamed into Brighton's new station in September 1841, the town has been the first choice for people from the capital wanting a day by the seaside.

Graham Greene captures the mood of Bank Holiday visitors at the beginning of *Brighton Rock*: 'They came in by train

from Victoria every five minutes, rocked down Queen's Road standing on top of the little local trams, stepped off in bewildered multitudes into fresh and glittering air.'

In 1750 there was nothing here but a decaying little fishing town with 2,000 inhabitants called Brighthelmstone – what is now the chic magnet for shoppers called The Lanes – but then Dr Richard Russell of Lewes published his treatise on the benefit of bathing in (and drinking) seawater. It meant rebirth for the town and the population rose from about 7,000 in 1800 to more than 20,000 two decades later.

The charismatic and fun-loving Prince Regent added the final seal of fashionable approval by having his fantastic Indo-Chinese palace built here, and the 'quality' flocked in his wake to enjoy the seasonal round of the baths, theatre, racecourse and assembly rooms. Grand seafront terraces and squares sprang up and the Victorians continued the love affair with Brighton, notably by building her two piers. The Palace Pier is one of the leading tourist venues in the country but the older and more beautiful West Pier fell into ruin and awaits massive renovation plans to come to fruition.

Jewel in the crown has to be 'Prinny's' Royal Pavilion, variously described as 'the most beautiful place in the world' and 'a collection of stone pumpkins and pepper boxes'. But it is surely too bizarre a building to come within the normal rules of architectural criticism.

The West Pier

Looking towards Brighton from the pier

FROM LEWES TO THE DISTANT HORIZON

For Lewes Town like Heaven is,
And Heaven is like Lewes Town.
Sheila Kaye-Smith, *St Peter and St Paul, The Gate of Lewes*

What a view Ditchling Beacon affords of the 'dim blue goodness of the Weald' with Surrey, and perhaps a chunk of Kent, forming the distant horizon. The beacon is a popular vantage point because it can be reached by car, but if you want to escape the madding crowd the South Downs Way will take you east and west.

Nearby is Plumpton Plain on the downland summit, from which the view is so lovely that it must be savoured – or woe betide you:

> *'He who gallops o'er Plumpton Plain*
> *Deserves n'er to gallop again.'*

Looking down on Lewes

Further east still, beyond the woody crown of Black Cap, the Downs fall gently to the 'gap town' of Lewes, historic guardian of the River Ouse where it bisects the hills.

The Norman castle dominates the county town and the High Street, which clings to a spine of a steep downland spur, is lined with old buildings in a variety of styles and materials. Plunging away to the south are a series of narrow streets, or twittens, leading towards the ruins of a once mighty Cluniac priory.

It's a town with an architectural delight at almost every turn, and from everywhere within it the gentle slopes of the Downs never seem far away. Notable features are Keere Street, largest of the twittens, with its central paving of 'petrified kidneys', or water-rolled flints, down whose precipitous length the Prince Regent is said to have driven a coach and four for a wager; and Southover Grange, boyhood home of the diarist John Evelyn (1620–1706), which incorporates Caen stone 'quarried' from the priory ruins.

Anne of Cleves House was never occupied by Henry VIII's fourth wife, though she drew an annual rent of seven shillings and sixpence from the property. It is now a museum.

The view from the edge of East Sussex at Ditchling Beacon

BY HORAM, HALLAND AND HEATHFIELD

I will go north about the shaws
And the deep ghylls that breed
Huge oaks and old, the which we hold
No more than Sussex weed . . .
Rudyard Kipling, *Sussex*

Fletching church stands at the head of a village street that is as perfect as you will encounter anywhere in the county, a medley of styles and vintages that rewards walking its length and back again.

Simon de Montfort and his army camped here on the eve of the Battle of Lewes in 1264, and supposedly spent the night in vigil before making their way through the dawn countryside to victory on the Downs above the county town, wresting power from Henry III.

East of Fletching lies Halland, a place made famous by the Bentley Wildfowl and Motor Museum. Here a massive range of feathered friends from all over the world can be viewed alongside vintage and veteran vehicles including a handsome cream and brown Bentley which has appeared in two films and was once driven by the actor David Niven.

Further east still and you encounter Horam, an area firmly on the map of anyone who likes a drink or two. Merrydown makes Sussex cider like nobody else, and the rich soil of these parts has also seen triumphant results in growing grapes. At St George's Vineyard in Waldron the English wine industry made such a name for itself internationally that big orders flooded in from as far afield as Japan.

Vines grow at Horam

To the north lie Heathfield and Old Heathfield, two communities separated by centuries and by the walled acres of Heathfield Park. One of the rites of spring in the county is that, no matter where they happen to be, Sussex folk always hear the first cuckoo on April 14th. The legendary old woman of 'Heffle Fair' would release the bird from her basket on that day to mark the start of wheeling and dealing among the horse trading gipsies who travelled here from all over the south for the annual spring market.

The view south they may or may not have noticed. But it has barely changed since Thomas Turner painted *The Vale of Heathfield* two centuries ago.

The picturesque village of Fletching

THE ROMANCE OF STEAM

Floreat Vapor!
'Long Live Steam!'

Doctor Beeching swung his famous axe in 1958 and the Lewes to East Grinstead service of British Rail ceased to exist. But a determined band of steam enthusiasts immediately formed a preservation society and battled for funds to buy a portion of the line. Many difficulties had to be overcome but eventually they acquired five miles, linking the defunct stations of Sheffield Park and Horsted Keynes. It became an instant tourist attraction, the romance of steam drawing thousands to ride in vintage rolling stock through some of the loveliest countryside this part of the county has to offer.

The Bluebell was the first volunteer-run railway to operate passenger trains. With only two engines and two carriages in the first season in 1960, the collection has grown to more than 30 steam locomotives and more than 100 carriages and wagons. The special atmosphere of a gentle scenic chug is enjoyed by more than 100,000 visitors every year.

The extent of the line has grown, too, in recent years now pushing up country as far as Kingscote. Plans are in hand to extend to East Grinstead, where there's a mainline station, giving the tantalising prospect of a mid-Sussex commuter being able to travel to London and back by steam and diesel.

Horsted Keynes station, dating from the late 19th century, is huge in size, magnificent in architecture and set in the middle of absolutely nowhere. It is as far removed from the village from which it takes its name as the smaller community of Danehill, a

Charming Danehill

place of charming cottages and a much-lamented lost pub with the unusual name of The Crocodile.

It must have been the glory days for hired trap drivers in the Victorian and Edwardian eras when country people were compelled to travel a minimum of three miles to reach their local station.

The Bluebell Line attracts thousands of visitors each year

THE MAGIC OF SHEFFIELD PARK

The spot that is dearer to me than the rest of the three kingdoms.
Edward Gibbon

Season's delights at Sheffield Park

One hundred gorgeous acres, man and nature working in perfect harmony. It was around 1775 that John Baker Holroyd, later the first Earl of Sheffield, employed the great Lancelot 'Capability' Brown to make something dramatic of the already scenic landscape here and the two lakes furthest from the house with their connecting cascade were his handiwork.

The two nearer lakes, linked by the 25 foot waterfall, date from the late 19th century when the third Earl added many exotic trees to Brown's native species.

Arthur Soames, who bought the property on the death of the Earl in 1909, then spent 25 years extending the collections of shrubs and trees – there are almost 200 kinds of conifer alone – that make this one of the National Trust's top attractions anywhere in the country.

There are two particularly magical periods at Sheffield Park: spring when the rhododendrons and azaleas are in bloom; and autumn, when the glowing reds, yellows and oranges of the dying leaves make a fluttering mosaic in the water's reflection.

The Cricket Field Plantation is on the site of the pitch laid out by the cricket-crazy third Earl, where the first ever match between England and Australia was played. It was customary for many years for the Aussies to play the first match of their tour at Sheffield Park against Lord Sheffield's XI; the great Dr W. G. Grace being one of the illustrious names to turn out for the home side. To this day, the Australian states compete for the Sheffield Shield.

The Neo-Gothic castellations of the privately-owned house, with a massive arched window at one end, are a recurring view as you wander the garden's paths. It was here that Edward Gibbon wrote *The Decline and Fall of the Roman Empire*.

Glimpses of the privately-owned house accompany a walk through Sheffield Park

ASHDOWN FOREST'S OPEN ACRES

Here birds and beasts, the timid populations,
Take shelter shy; beneath a sky of greenery with gladsome
revelations –
This is God's sanctuary, here He passeth by.
E. W. Orne Ward, *A Sussex Sanctuary*

This is no forest. There are belts of woodland, to be sure, but the real glory of Ashdown is its openness – acre upon acre of heathland rolling across the Weald.

This was a forest in the Norman sense, a vast hunting chase which was enclosed, sometime before the end of the 13th century, by a fenced bank which prevented the red and fallow deer from escaping. John of Gaunt, who held the forest from 1372 to 1399, was one of its most ardent huntsmen.

The great ironmasters coppiced large areas of Ashdown Forest to feed their furnaces. But the Commoners successfully resisted the attempts of powerful landowners to enclose the area (and so take away their rights to graze animals on the waste, cut bracken for bedding, and fell birches for firewood, fencing and building of their homes). In 1693 the law came down in their favour – a Royal Commission awarding them 6,400 acres which is the very area of breezy tracts of heath and scrub open to the public today.

It's a tousled landscape of ling, gorse and purple moorgrass which conservationists preserve today through a never-ending programme of cutting back the scrub and bracken and weeding out the invasive silver birch and Scots pine. The forest, constituting five per cent of Britain's remaining lowland heath, is

Morning sunlight in the forest

designated as a Site of Special Scientific Interest within an Area of Outstanding Natural Beauty.

As Ben Darby put it, in *Journey Through the Weald:* 'No matter how often you go there, it always seems new, and always a place apart. The Forest does not claim you, and you not claim the Forest. You are always a visitor. But it fascinates. It is irresistible.'

The open heathland of Ashdown Forest, towards the Weald

HOME OF A HONEY-LOVING BEAR

So off they went together. But wherever they go, and whatever happens to them on the way, in that enchanted place on the top of the forest a little boy and his bear will always be playing.
A. A. Milne, *The House at Pooh Corner*

Is there one place in the county that surpasses all others? The writer E. V. Lucas certainly implied so when he described Withyham as the Jewel of Sussex.

It is not so much the nature of the village that makes it so special – in fact it is rather spread out – as the sheer charm of the rolling landscape in which it lies. If there's a heart to Withyham it has to be the church. The steep climb up to it, with its view across a lake to Hartfield's spire piercing the distant woodland, is worth getting out of breath for. The building contains many memorials to the Sackville and de la Warr families, the most impressive being Caius Cibber's sculptured monument to Thomas Sackville, who died in 1677 at the age of just 13.

Farmer Edward Frisby Howis certainly loved Withyham so much that he stated in his will that he should have a spy hole in his grave to look out across his acres at Sunnyford Farm. A length of drainpipe served the purpose when the good farmer was laid to rest in the early years of the 19th century.

A little bear with a liking for honey has to a large extent dwarfed the picturesque qualities of Hartfield. A. A. Milne lived at Cotchford Farm on the edge of the village and set his stories of Winnie the Pooh and his son Christopher on the high hills and in Ashdown Forest. Today, 'the enchanted places' like Pooh Corner, Poohsticks Bridge and Galleons Lap have become places of

Pooh Corner at Hartfield

pilgrimage for fans the world over.

E. H. Shepard, whose drawings are inseparable from Milne's text, shares a monument with him at Gills Lap, the famous Galleons Lap of the stories, a typical forest high spot with wonderful extensive views.

Spring in Withyham

SPORTSMEN OLD AND NEW

Flew over leagues of whispering wonder,
Fairy forests and flowery palaces.
Alfred Noyes, *The Tramp Transfigured*

White figures on the village green . . . a timeless vision of England. It could be anywhere, but this is Frant, high in its corner of the county, where a mighty clout from a batsman would be Kent's problem, not Sussex's.

This was a great sporting community, though there are many in these conservation-conscious times who would be horrified to know that otters in the local streams were a principal quarry of the huntsmen, and that one family kept a pack of terriers for hunting badgers in the 1920s.

It is many years since the last 'Fawn Supper', when the Marquess of Abergavenny gave a fawn each year to be cooked for the employees on his estate as a Christmas feast.

The distinctive crest depicting a bull of the Nevill family, Earls and Marquesses of Abergavenny, adorns many of the houses in these parts for Eridge Park is the seat of this leading Sussex family. They have owned Eridge since at least 1300 and Queen Elizabeth I stayed at a hunting lodge here in 1573.

The house was remodelled into a vast Gothic castle by the second Earl in 1810, who renamed it Eridge Castle and made it his chief residence after Kidbrooke Park, near East Grinstead. It once had 70 miles of rides and drives. The castle was demolished in 1938 and the modern house which replaced it has been reduced to one third of its original size and is now known by its original name of Eridge Park.

Misty morning at Eridge

They make good use of the rugged terrain and rocky outcrops at Eridge, where there is an outdoor pursuits centre. Among other things you can learn mountaineering and canoeing.

On the village green at Frant

East Sussex is a county with everything. In his evocative photographs, David Sellman seeks to reflect the county in all its moods and colours: from the golden hues of autumn, the white frosts of winter and the gentle greens of spring to the blaze of the summer sun. The text by Sussex newspaper man, Rupert Taylor, chronicles the county's history and demonstrates just how much it has to offer today, both to local people and visitors alike.

David Sellman first started taking photos at the age of ten, using a Kodak Brownie and then a Zeiss Ikonta, at that time on black and white film. On leaving school he worked in a studio in London's West End where he learnt about photography as a profession and his duties included assisting Cecil Beaton, sometimes on royal sittings. After ten years in London he moved to a firm in the Kent countryside and became a photographic colour printer producing giant photographic enlargements for film backgrounds. The outdoor life beckoned and he turned to landscape photography, first in Kent and Sussex, and then nationwide. Now his time is split between shooting for his library and commissioned work for clients. All work is now in colour and cameras used are a Mamiya and a Wista.

Rupert Taylor lives in Uckfield and is deputy editor of the *Sussex Express*. He is the author of a number of popular books on the county including *The East Sussex Village Book*.

Front cover photograph: Winton, near Alfriston
Back cover photograph: Sunset at Hastings